ELVIS PRESLE

A Life From Beginning to End

Copyright © 2018 by Hourly History.

All rights reserved.

Table of Contents

Introduction
Elvis and His Twin
The Start of His Music Career
That's All Right
Early Hits
Presley's Controversial Rise
Elvis Joins the Army
Military Years
The King of Rock Returns
Comeback in Las Vegas
Last Years and Death
Conclusion

Introduction

Elvis Presley was much more than a cultural icon; he was a reliable barometer of the world he grew up in. Long before the cultural revolutions of the '60s and '70s, Elvis was sparking a dynastic change of hands in American society. And by his own admission, much of it was by accident. Whenever his performances caused a stir, Elvis was always the first to ask what all the fuss was about. When questioned if he was trying to provoke a response from his audience, Elvis innocently replied that he was just doing what came naturally.

According to Elvis, as much as James Dean was a "rebel without a cause," he was a rebel completely by accident. If we believe him, everything he did that led to his rise to stardom was just some sort of cosmic alignment of happenstance. Elvis claimed that when he went into Sun Records to record what would be his first song, he wasn't looking to become famous; he maintained that he just wanted to record a song for his mom's birthday.

There are still those that argue that Elvis knew exactly what he was doing and was a slick mastermind of manipulation when it came to pop culture. But whatever the case may be, Elvis led a life that was unapparelled. Call it fate, or call it dogged perseverance, he remade the world in his image. Learn about the life, the legend, and the unmistakable icon—Elvis Presley.

Chapter One

Elvis and His Twin

"Rock and roll music, if you like it, if you feel it, you can't help but move to it. That's what happens to me. I can't help it."

—Elvis Presley

The man who would be known as the "King of Rock and Roll" was born a relative pauper, in Tupelo, Mississippi, on January 8, 1935. His mother Gladys didn't have enough money for hospitals or doctors, so she gave birth to Elvis right in her and her husband Vernon's modest home. It was in such threadbare circumstances that women often encountered difficulties in their pregnancies and Gladys was no exception.

As soon as her baby arrived, she was saddened to find it already dead; the child was stillborn. But Gladys was in for a surprise because no sooner than she gave birth to the first lifeless baby, another one was eagerly on its way out. Since Gladys had never been examined by a physician prior to going into labor, she had no way of knowing that she wasn't expecting just one baby, but two.

Gladys and her husband prayed with all their might that the second child would live. Elvis Aron Presley was born just seconds apart from his dead brother. The deceased child would be posthumously named Jesse Garon, and though Elvis never got to be properly introduced to his sibling, the death of his twin would haunt him for the rest of his life. It is said that starting as a small child, he would visit his brother's gravesite on a regular basis.

Even after all his fortune and fame, Elvis was known to make offhanded mention of his brother as if he were a major part of his existence. But in reality, he was an only child and would remain so for the rest of his life. Soon after the complications of the twin delivery, Gladys was informed that she most likely would not be able to bear any more children. And so, Elvis' fate as a brother-less young man was sealed.

Without any siblings, Elvis grew greatly attached to his parents, and most especially his mother whom he often looked upon as his playmate. As his father was out and about searching for work during the depths of the Great Depression of the 1930s, Elvis and his mom were often left to their own machinations. Being her only child, Gladys was fiercely protective of Elvis and would stop at nothing to make sure he didn't get hurt.

This protectiveness was on full display when Elvis first became old enough to go to school. She struggled to let him go but finally relented, as long as she could walk him there and back, holding his hand the entire way. While other children may have shunned such an overbearing parent, Elvis seemed to relish the attention. And to maximize this attention, Elvis learned to be a performer from an early age.

It was this need for attention and approval that led Elvis to join the choir at the local Assembly of God Church that he and his parents attended. These Sunday forays with singing then led him to try out for a local fair on October 3, 1945. Elvis finished as the runner-up. His family was impressed enough with the result that they ended up pooling their resources to buy the young Elvis a guitar for his birthday.

He actually wanted a new bicycle, but that guitar would soon take Elvis Presley places that even the shiniest, fanciest bicycle never could. After being given his first guitar, Elvis took it with him wherever he went. By this time he had entered the sixth grade, and he could always be seen accompanied by the guitar—which seemed much larger in comparison to his slim figure—slung over his back. He was determined to learn how to play the instrument.

His mother, recognizing his passion, enlisted the new pastor in town, a man by the name of Frank Smith, to give Elvis some basic guitar lessons. But the tenacious Elvis wasn't going to sit around and wait for someone to teach him, he was already learning much on his own. He had acquired a book on finger charts and guitar chords, which he had studied quite extensively, teaching himself how his hands should be positioned on the fretboard.

Yet it was a friendship young Elvis had made in the classroom with a student named James Ausborn that brought him the most promise in his new field of study. This classmate just happened to be the younger brother of a man who was already a local music legend, known by the moniker of Mississippi Slim. Slim's real name was Carvel Lee Ausborn; he was a country singer and radio personality for Tupelo, Mississippi's WELO broadcast station. Elvis was introduced to the local hero, and Slim was soon impressed with what he perceived to be Presley's already burgeoning talent.

Slim soon thereafter had young Elvis booked for a live appearance on his radio show to perform a song. But when the time came for Elvis to make his debut on the airwaves, he found himself suddenly beset with a terrible case of stage fright. He had to postpone his appearance, but he did manage to get it together enough to engage in a live performance during the next week's program. At the tender age of 12, this live session with WELO radio would mark the beginning of a lifelong career.

Chapter Two

The Start of His Music Career

"Since the beginning, it was just the same. The only difference, the crowds are bigger now."

—Elvis Presley

Elvis was sent packing on one of the biggest moves of his life in November 1948, when the family moved some 100 miles north to Memphis, Tennessee. With the clothes on their back and not much else, the Presleys piled into Vernon's 1939 Plymouth and hit the road. Upon their arrival, they stayed in cheap rooming houses until Vernon was able to gain employment for a paint company and Gladys a job in a textile mill making curtains, scraping together enough money to get a place of their own.

They moved into a two-bedroom apartment called the Lauderdale Courts and also found a new church in their new surroundings. Here Elvis befriended Jesse Lee, the son of the church pastor, who was also a fellow music aficionado. Jesse soon became a regular visitor at the Presley home, often giving Elvis guitar lessons and even engaging in impromptu performances with him in the laundry room for whoever would listen to them.

From here, Elvis networked with the Memphis music scene further, making many friends and partnerships as he entered high school. He soon began to attend parties and social get-togethers held by his peers. At these social gatherings, Elvis became widely known for his abilities as a musician.

But not everyone at L.C. Humes High School was so enthused about Elvis' talent. When he was in the eighth grade, his music teacher famously gave him a C in music class, promptly informing him he had no real ability when it came to singing. Elvis, feeling misunderstood, protested at the snobbery of his teacher and informed her that she had it all wrong about him and music. He then arrived at the next class session with his guitar and performed a rendition of "Keep Them Cold Icy Fingers Off Me" to show his instructor just where he was coming from musically. As a result, the music teacher is said to have come to an agreement with Elvis, as she sarcastically informed him that he was right when he had complained that she didn't appreciate his "kind of singing."

Someone who did appreciate the stylings of the young Elvis, however, was a young man named Jesse Lee Denson. Jesse, too, was a Tennessee transplant and arrived a year before Elvis. Denson first encountered Elvis when he witnessed one of Gladys' many relapses into her habit of walking her son to school. Denson thought this to be extremely odd, and his curiosity piqued, he confronted Elvis about the situation. Denson then soon convinced Elvis that he needed to persuade his mom not to walk him to school in order to save his reputation.

The opening to pry his mother's overbearing hands lose came when she had an unexpected doctor's appointment. Due to the appointment, she would be unable to walk Elvis to school. It was then that Denson, who was larger and a couple of years older, volunteered to walk Elvis to the school grounds. From then on, according to Denson, he became Elvis' bodyguard. Denson also became Elvis' first band member. Denson introduced him to the Burnette brothers, Dorsey and Johnny, forming what would become a quartet.

When he wasn't in school or playing music, Elvis was seeking to raise himself out of poverty by working part-time jobs as an usher at the local movie theatre and at various factories around Tennessee. With his extra cash, he was able to buy new clothes and as his wardrobe changed, so did his confidence. By his senior year of high school, Elvis had overcome much of his previous stage fright and began to play music outside of his home.

One of the first of these gigs was a stint at his high school's talent show. Elvis would continue his courtship of music off and on, and shortly after graduating from school at age 18 in August 1953, Elvis decided to pay a visit to Sun Studios, the brainchild of promoter and music mogul Sam Phillips. Although Sun Studios was an up and coming label, it is said that Elvis came knocking on their door with the most innocent of intentions; he wanted to record a song for his mother's birthday.

Elvis had paid in advance—three dollars and ninety-eight cents worth of recording time—and he was ready to make music. The song he wished to record was an old, traditional ballad called "My Happiness" which he knew was a favorite of his mother's. Phillips' partner at the studio, a woman named Marion Keisker, was working the main desk when Elvis came in. Intrigued by the young man, she began to ask him questions.

She asked, "What kind of music do you sing?" and Elvis replied simply, "I sing all kinds." She then inquired, "Who do you sound like?" At which Elvis emphatically informed her, "I don't sound like nobody!" After hearing his unique rendition of the old classic, Keisker was ready to agree with him. Impressed by his unique sound and ability, she took down his name for future reference. She knew that she didn't want to forget it.

Chapter Three

That's All Right

"I don't think I'm bad for people. If I did think I was bad for people, I would go back to driving a truck. And I really mean this."

—Elvis Presley

Shortly after graduating from high school in 1953, Elvis began to think about what he wanted to do with life. He loved music, but at this point, he didn't see it as much more than a hobby. He certainly didn't think that he could make a living off of it. Elvis, like so many of his peers, decided that he needed to learn a practical trade. He had no intention of going to college, so he went straight to work for the first company that would hire him: a local machine shop.

Elvis was working long hours, doing grueling manual labor, but as exhausting as it was, he still found enough strength to dream. And he found himself ever so slowly being pulled back toward the music he had momentarily spurned as being impractical. During the nights that he was able to get away from the machine shop, he attended gospel singalongs at his local church where he kept his singing ability primed and ready, just like he would a piece of machinery at the shop.

Then, at the suggestion of his good friend Ronnie Smith, Elvis tried out to be a vocalist for local musician Eddie Bond's latest band. Bond had been running the so-called rockabilly circuit for years and would later be associated not only with Elvis but also Roy Orbison and Johnny Cash. Bond was known for having an eye for talent, but whatever the case may be, his talent scouting ability must have been off on that particular night. After hearing Elvis audition, he categorically rejected him and even infamously advised him to drive a truck because he would never make it as a singer. History, of course, would prove Bond wrong.

Not long after this rejection, Sun Records would come calling. Phillips invited Elvis over to his studio, and with the help of studio musicians Winfield "Scotty" Moore and Bill Black, they got to work making music.

At first, it was tough going, and the trio just couldn't seem to connect with each other. After several hours, the group was ready to call it quits and go home. But right at the last minute when everyone was getting ready to walk out, Elvis abruptly picked up the guitar for one more song. He began to break into a spontaneous rendition of Arthur Crudup's classic "That's All Right." As much as he had struggled most of the night, suddenly with this one song Elvis was able to conquer his nerves and be himself.

And as he swayed with his guitar crooning, "That's alright mama—that's alright with you! That's alright mama, just anyway you do!" the other musicians turned back around and began playing along with him, suddenly perfectly in tune with Elvis' singing. Phillips, poking his head back into the studio, quickly realized that they were onto something and hit the record button, and the rest is music history.

Phillips, convinced he now had the next big thing, immediately called up the neighboring radio station and requested for them to put Elvis' recording on the air. A few days later, the station's DJ, Dewey, got a hold of the recording and played it during a segment called the "Red, Hot, and Blue" show. It was an immediate hit and had listeners calling in by the hundreds requesting that the song be played again. Elvis and his band then went back to the studio soon thereafter and recorded their next song together, "Blue Moon of Kentucky."

This song would become the B Side for "That's All Right." They then had the single pressed and released to the public. The music group was now ready to perform and went on the road on July 17, 1954, performing at the Bon Air Club. Elvis is said to have been so nervous during the performance that his legs shook when he played. The audience assumed that this was just all part of the act and screamed and cheered at the musician's gyrating hips. This would become a trademark of Elvis and a trait he would carry with him, even long after his case of the jitters had subsided.

Chapter Four

Early Hits

"Rhythm is something you either have or don't have. But when you have it, you have it all over."

—Elvis Presley

In the music circles of Tennessee, Elvis was making a name for himself, and on October 2, 1954, he was determined to make it with the biggest music venue in the state: Nashville Tennessee's Grand Ole Opry. The results were mixed to say the least, and after Elvis stepped down from the stage, the manager phoned Phillips and informed him that although he believed Elvis had talent, he was just not the right kind of act for the Opry.

Phillips took these remarks in stride, however, and had Elvis scheduled to perform for the Opry's biggest competitor on the block, the Louisiana Hayride. Based out of Shreveport, Louisiana, the Hayride was known to be a bit more edgy of a program than most of its contemporaries, and Phillips hoped that perhaps they could better incorporate Elvis' unique skill set into their repertoire.

Elvis was to perform over a live radio broadcast, but he had what amounted to a panic attack shortly into the performance and had to abort the session. Elvis soon recovered and was able to go back out and deliver a set that provoked cheers of excitement from the crowd. The Hayride was so impressed that they signed Elvis on to perform on a regular basis with routine Saturday night bookings on the program. Encouraged by this news, the first thing Elvis did was take his old, beaten up guitar and trade it in for a new one. He sold his old guitar for 8 bucks and paid $175 for a new Martin acoustic, the same type of instrument he would make famous later on.

Due to a heavy touring schedule and his routine appearances on radio shows like Hayride, Elvis was soon widely known throughout the American south. This renown brought Elvis to the attention of Colonel Tom Parker. In reality, the man was never a colonel, and his name was not even Tom Parker; this was simply a pseudonym that he had created. Colonel Parker was actually born in the Netherlands with the name of Andreas Cornelis van Kuijk. And although his coming to the United States is not exactly clear, it is widely believed that Colonel Parker emigrated at some point in the early 1920s. Parker then bounced around from odd job to odd job, before enlisting with the U.S. military.

It remains an enigma how an illegal alien such as Colonel Parker managed to join up with the U.S. Army in the first place, but he served for a few years until he was discharged. And while he was never a colonel in the armed forces, he thought that the title commanded authority. So, when he began his career as a promoter, he thought having a name like Colonel Parker would be a way to gain notoriety and get instant name recognition.

At the time he was introduced to Elvis, Parker's biggest act was a country music artist named Hank Snow. But after seeing Elvis, he believed that his fame could easily surpass that of Snow's, and he sought to place himself in the position of mentor in order to shape Elvis Presley's career.

Taking charge of the situation, Colonel Parker recruited Elvis to join up with Snow's upcoming tour. Parker worked to convince Elvis that he needed to break out of the regional scene of the south and tour in other parts of the country. He also convinced Elvis to part with Sun Records for a larger record company that could get him more airplay. Elvis was hesitant to break with his early backers, but after talking with his parents—his father Vernon seemed particularly taken by Parker's big talk of record and movie deals—Elvis was convinced that it would be for the best.

In August 1955, Colonel Parker obtained the title of special adviser—manager in everything but name—and had Elvis signed to RCA Records. The Colonel didn't disappoint in his deal-making and was able to negotiate a contract in which RCA paid out an advance salary of $30,000, which was an amount practically unheard of at the time for a brand new, untested recording artist. With his advance in his pocket, Elvis got to work.

It was on January 10, 1956, just a couple of days after his 21st birthday, that Elvis made music history once again. The first song he recorded for RCA was "Heartbreak Hotel." The song was brilliant for the time. It was initially a sad ballad about a messy breakup, but Elvis turned it into an upbeat rock anthem, with his voice rising and falling like the tides of the ocean; subdued in some parts but then roaring with life and enthusiasm in others.

The recording studio employed for the session was unique as well. This particular RCA facility was attached to a local Methodist Church in Nashville and not all sounds from the adjoining church could be insulated from the recordings. If you listen closely to the song, it is said that you can hear parishioners dropping change into a coke machine in the church lobby on the other side of the wall. The studio also had the unique feature of a large stairwell positioned in the back of the building that worked as a kind of echo chamber. This seemed to provide a stunning sound effect for the haunting "Heartbreak Hotel," making it sound as if Elvis' plaintive cries in the song were coming from deep down at the bottom of an abyss.

The song was an immediate hit, and 21-year-old Elvis Presley was now fast becoming a household name. With fame came money, and Elvis soon began to spend it. He wasn't afraid to splurge on his loved ones, and he famously bought his mother a pink Cadillac, as well as purchasing a new home for all of them to live in together. Yes, even though Elvis was a superstar known all across the nation, he still lived with his parents. But this was an arrangement of choice rather than necessity, and by sharing the good life with his family, Elvis felt he was granting them something that they had all been deprived for way too long.

Chapter Five
Presley's Controversial Rise

"People ask me where I got my singing style. I didn't copy my style from anybody."

—Elvis Presley

By late 1955, Elvis was getting wide-ranging radio play, but he still had his detractors. The biggest problem with Elvis' breakout success was that most in the music business didn't know what category that his unique sound should be placed in. Even though his music had some country overtones, the country music station didn't want to touch it, because there was too much of a blues influence.

And yet there was often a problem with the blues stations too, who rejected Elvis for sounding too much like a "hillbilly." It was this pejorative that lent Presley's music its first tentative title of "rockabilly," a term that would later evolve into the more familiar, "rock and roll."

Elvis completed his first full-length album on March 23, 1956, which continued his eclectic mix of country, blues, and pop. The album surpassed all expectations and became the first to sell over a million copies. Following close on the heels of this success, Elvis went back to the studio and recorded the songs "Hound Dog" and "Don't

Be Cruel," which quickly became the most successful two-sided record in history. And on April 3, 1956, Presley performed on the *Milton Berle Show*, a live variety broadcast on NBC. Shortly thereafter Elvis released the single for "Heartbreak Hotel," and it went number one on the charts.

Elvis returned to the *Milton Berle Show* on June 5, where he performed the previous blues hit "Hound Dog." His rendition received rave reviews from many, but a few were not too pleased. The *New York Times* published an op-ed piece in which Elvis was lambasted as having "no discernible singing ability—his phrasing, if it can be called that, consisted of the stereotyped variations that go with a beginner's aria in a bathtub."

Another writer, Ben Gross of the *Daily News* concurred with these harsh critiques, writing that, "Elvis, who rotates his pelvis, gave an exhibition that was suggestive and vulgar, tinged with the kind of animalism that should be confined to dives and bordellos." Soon after these critiques, Elvis acquired the derisive nickname that would stick with him for the rest of his life, "Elvis the Pelvis" Presley.

Elvis cringed at such expressions and viewed it as nothing short of schoolyard bullying. He responded to his detractors, calling their taunts out as "one of the most childish expressions I ever heard, coming from an adult." Despite these harsh remarks from the press over his live broadcasts, Elvis was still in high demand in TV land. Soon he would be called upon to perform on *The Ed Sullivan Show*.

The Ed Sullivan Show was the premier variety show of the day, and it was hands down one of the most popular programs on television. This was a show that caused big stars to get even bigger. The only problem was that Sullivan, too, had his own misgivings about Elvis Presley, at one point declaring him "unfit for family viewing." But the demand soon outweighed even Ed Sullivan's dismay, and Elvis was booked to perform on the live broadcast scheduled for September 9, 1956.

As fate would have it, when the time came for Elvis to perform on the program, Sullivan himself would be a no-show. He had gotten into a bad car accident just days before and was still recuperating. Filling in for Ed Sullivan was actor Charles Laughton, who served as guest host. Elvis triumphantly marched onto the stage in his plaid jacket and suede shoes, greeting his screaming fans by telling them that "this is probably the greatest honor I have ever had in my life." After making this candid announcement, Elvis gave the signal and he and his band immediately burst into "Don't be Cruel."

In order to avoid the previous controversy over Elvis' pelvis, the camera mainly focused above his waist, zooming in on his face or panning to his backup singers. But even so, the wild screams of his fans still punctuated all of those gyrating moves that were being made off camera, a fact that Elvis acknowledged in between songs by telling them, "Thank you, ladies!"

In regard to the songs, the most memorable tune was no doubt "Love Me Tender." This song was to be the title track of the movie of the same name that Elvis had just begun to work on. It was an instant success. Even as he was performing it for the first time in front of an audience, radio DJs all over the nation were recording copies of the live performance so that they could play teasers on their radio shows the next day.

This hype generated massive interest and led to a tidal wave of pre-release orders before the official track even came out. And on top of all this free publicity, Colonel Parker had arranged that Elvis be paid no less than $50,000 from this one appearance on *The Ed Sullivan Show*, which was an astounding amount in those days. Elvis Presley, whom Ed Sullivan had considered a disgrace, was vindicated by this success. But, the recriminations of the older generation were not over yet.

Shortly after Elvis' appearance on the show, crowds of concerned citizens began to burn the likeness of Elvis Presley in effigy. Most notably was the spontaneous display on the campus of Notre Dame High School in St. Louis, Missouri, where huge piles of Elvis records, photographs, posters, and even teddy bears were burned in what was termed a "bonfire of the vanities."

But even as his likeness was going up in smoke, Elvis' esteem would only continue to rise.

Chapter Six
Elvis Joins the Army

"I'm trying to keep a level head. You have to be careful out in the world. It's so easy to get turned."

—Elvis Presley

In October 1956, Elvis released his second studio album, the self-titled *Elvis* or, as it has been more widely known, *Elvis Presley No. 2*. With Elvis reprising classic hits such as "Old Shep" and "Ready Teddy," the album was soon selling like wildfire. It has been widely noted that Elvis was not much of a songwriter and mostly retooled the songs of others. Some criticize him because of this fact. But even though Elvis may not have been the originator of some of these songs, he certainly knew how to make an original approach.

In late 1956, Elvis' manager Colonel Parker envisioned Presley's star emblazoned on the big screen. Elvis' first feature-length film, *Love Me Tender*, hit the box office on November 15, 1956. And one year after movie legend and counterculture icon James Dean's death, Elvis was in many ways billed as a suitable replacement.

But the setting of the film, taking place during the Civil War with Elvis playing the part of farmhand turned musician, seemed a bit removed from the counterculture of the 1950s. Without any professional training or acting experience, Elvis was a little wary of playing the role at first, but Colonel Parker insisted on it, believing that they could gain a lot of notoriety and—perhaps most important for the Colonel—a lot of money.

This film and all of Elvis' later films have been widely lambasted as dull B movies of the first order, but when *Love Me Tender* came out it was a box office success. Elvis was more serious about his acting career than many realize, even toying with the idea of attending classes at the Actor's Studio. This focus on acting, however, soon took away from Elvis' efforts in music, and he began to have less and less time for recording new songs and touring.

Soon it seemed as if Elvis' whole purpose for music became simply to make soundtracks for his latest films. But even so, releases such as "Teddy Bear," "Too Much," and "All Shook Up" in early 1957 all managed to go to the number one spot.

It was with his simultaneous earnings from music and film that Elvis was able to purchase a certain property in West Tennessee by the name of Graceland. Presley paid $102,500 for the farmhouse styled mansion and its surrounding acres on March 19, 1957. The house was huge, and the land outside its windows gave Elvis ample space to shield him and his entourage from the fans that were always threatening to encircle them. At Elvis' previous residence, a more modest home in Tennessee, masses of fans had begun waiting outside for the King all hours of the day and night, blocking roads and creating quite a nuisance for him and the neighbors. This wouldn't be a problem at Graceland.

This 13.8-acre estate in Memphis, Tennessee had plenty of room for Elvis and his friends and family to roam around in. But Elvis wouldn't spend a lot of time at his new home before the U.S. draft board began to seek him out. You see, back in the 1950s, it was a rule that all able-bodied men between the ages of 18 and 25 were eligible for mandatory conscription into the United States armed forces.

Elvis' number in this massive draft lottery came up right around the Christmas of 1957, and he was promptly alerted of his upcoming summoning to the U.S. Army. Even though 1957 was a time of peace between the Korean and the Vietnam wars, it was still considered an essential part of America's contingency plan to have a ready force of trained troops at all times.

Elvis always knew that being drafted was a possibility and had hoped to avoid it. But nevertheless, when Uncle Sam came calling, Elvis Presley duly responded. He was scheduled for a pre-induction physical exam on January 4, 1957, at the Kennedy Veterans Hospital in Memphis, Tennessee. In order for Elvis to be officially placed within the army, he had to pass the standard mental and physical exam.

So, if Elvis wished to cheat the system and claim he had severe asthma and flat feet so he would be declared unfit for service, this was his opportunity to do so. But Elvis approached the testing as honestly as he could and passed all aspects of the examination without any trouble.

He was classified in the official paperwork as an "A Profile" which meant that he was in prime physical condition and an ideal candidate for the draft. This meant that he could be drafted at any time.

Elvis seemed to accept his fate, and several weeks later when reporters inquired with him on the subject, he simply said, "I haven't heard anything from them since I took my physical. When I do go, I don't expect any favors from them. I'll just do what they tell me." In the meantime, Elvis finished up filming the movie *Jailhouse Rock* and recording the subsequent hit songs to go with it.

It was while he was busy with these simultaneous projects that Elvis received his official draft notice. He was notified that he was to report on base December 19, 1957. Presley, the King of Rock and Roll, now had to line up with all the other recruits and remain under strict army control for the next two years.

Chapter Seven

Military Years

"As a person he was wonderful. He really was a great person. He was full of life. He had a great sense of humor. Very talented, of course, but very caring to his parents. There was a very endearing quality about Elvis."

—Priscilla Presley

Some say that the stress of having her only son shipped off to the military was too much for Gladys Presley to handle; the stress of it made her ill. In retrospect, such things are hard to confirm. But the truth of the matter is that shortly after Elvis' arrival at basic training in Fort Hood, Texas, Gladys did indeed come down with an abrupt sickness and was diagnosed with an advanced stage of hepatitis in early August 1958.

Upon hearing the news, Elvis requested and was given temporary leave to see her. But sadly enough, on August 14, just two days after her son's arrival, she passed away. This was an earth-shattering blow to Elvis who considered his mother his best friend. She was his confidant, the one he trusted more than any other. He would call her at all hours of the night and day just to get her opinion on his various struggles in life.

He didn't know how to go on without that vital part of his existence no longer intact. Losing her, Elvis felt like he had lost a major piece of his world, and some say that he never recovered from the loss. The very next morning after her passing, Elvis was found by paparazzi on the front steps of his home in Graceland crying his eyes out. Instead of showing any decency or compassion, as Elvis buried his head in his hands with tears streaming through the cracks of his fingers, the reporters hurled insensitive questions as cameras flashed all around him.

Elvis did have some sincere well-wishers, however, and shortly after his mother's death he received a tidal wave of support from regular fans and fellow superstars alike. Among the latter camp, he received several telegrams from the likes of Dean Martin, Marlon Brando, Ricky Nelson, and Sammy Davis Jr., all wishing him the best.

When the time came for Elvis' mother to be laid down in her final resting place, the cemetery is said to have been overflowing with 500 fans and well-wishers. In the next few days afterward, Elvis was mostly inconsolable, shifting between fits of uncontrollable grief and long, morose talks of all the good times he had had with his mother.

Considering the circumstances, the army extended Elvis' leave to five more days. Those extra days of sadness wouldn't do much for him, and after his leave came to a close on October 1, 1958, the still grieving King of Rock was unceremoniously shuffled off to Friedberg, Germany to finish his training. Elvis was initially trained just like any soldier, but it soon became apparent that he wouldn't always be treated impartially.

Instead of staying in the military barracks with the other soldiers on the base, he was soon granted permission to stay at private hotels instead. Elvis managed to adjust to his new routine, and as he busied himself with his work on the base, he managed to overcome much of his grief. He began to enjoy his time on the base, and a regular group of friends started to hang out with him at his hotel where they would have boisterous get-togethers.

These gatherings became famous for Elvis' love of squirt guns, and the group would often hold squirt gun battles right in the hotel lobby. As you could imagine, the proprietors of this hotel didn't take too kindly to these antics and soon requested for Elvis and his entourage to go somewhere else. He obliged them by packing his bags and renting a nearby house.

As much fun as Elvis was having with his friends, his all-night benders were beginning to catch up with him, and he was soon becoming too tired to do his daily duties on the base. It was due to this tiredness that one of his army buddies introduced him to amphetamines, encouraging Elvis to pop pills to stay awake. Elvis loved the way the pills made him feel, and unfortunately, this would serve as the basis of a lifelong addiction to drugs.

Elvis would also gain some healthy interests while he was overseas. One of which was a passion for martial arts, of which he would become an enduring enthusiast. It was the famed German instructor Jurgen Seydel who enrolled Elvis at his local karate club. Presley was said to be a natural and a studious student, attaining his black belt before he was discharged from the service. He would hold a love of karate for the rest of his life.

Around this same time period, Elvis would meet another lifelong love: a girl named Priscilla. She was the step-daughter of an air force captain who was stationed at the same base as Presley. Elvis met Priscilla on September 13, 1959, when she came to a get-together for the troops that was being held at Elvis' home. He is said to have been instantly enamored with Priscilla and talked with her late into the night.

Pricilla's parents were at first frustrated with the singer's interest in their daughter. She was only 14 at the time, and Elvis was 24. A relationship between them would be considered off limits—if not illegal—by today's standards. But Elvis talked to Priscilla's step-father and explained that his interest in her was benign, and he promised not to make any serious advances toward a relationship until she was older.

A few months later, Elvis was discharged from the military, and in March 1960, he returned to the United States. By the time he came back, society was in a state of great transition. It was an election year; President Dwight D. Eisenhower was scheduled to leave office, succeeded by either Richard Nixon or John F. Kennedy. The Civil Rights Movement was picking up speed, and a group of fresh-faced British rock and roll rivals called the Beatles were on the verge of taking the U.S. by storm.

The King had returned, but his kingdom was not the same.

Chapter Eight
The King of Rock Returns

"A live concert to me is exciting because of all the electricity that is generated in the crowd and on stage. It's my favorite part of the business, live concerts."

—Elvis Presley

Elvis Presley arrived back on American soil on March 2, 1960, and received his honorable discharge from service on March 5. He then got on a train that took him from New Jersey all the way to Tennessee. After arriving back in Graceland, Elvis took a couple of days to catch his breath before calling his old friends in music to plot his next move. On March 20, with his old crew back in order, Elvis and his mates hopped into a car and drove to Nashville, where they soon set to work at RCA's studio to pick up where they had left off.

With no time wasted, a new album was quickly put together from which the single "Stuck on You" was gleaned and immediately handed over to the radio stations where it gained traction on the music charts, going all the way to number one. After finishing up in the studio, Elvis boarded a train to film a comeback special as the guest of honor for Frank Sinatra's variety show called the *Frank Sinatra Timex Special*.

It was rather strange that Sinatra agreed to do the show since in the past the two had been rivals, and Sinatra had on occasion even been antagonistic to Presley in particular and rock and roll in general. He had once summed up rock music as being "sung, played and written for the most part by cretinous goons." But cretinous or not, by the time of Elvis' return in 1960, Sinatra agreed to pay him $125,000 just to play a walk-on role on his show.

As it turns out, Sinatra's ratings had been suffering, and being ever the shrewd businessman, he knew that Elvis re-emerging after two years absence on his program would cause his ratings to shoot through the roof. Sinatra was right, millions tuned in to watch as Elvis walked on stage in his military dress to greet a cheering crowd. Soon after this initial skit, Elvis emerged on stage in a tuxedo and sang a duet with Sinatra's daughter, Nancy Sinatra, before performing with Frank himself, including a duet on the hit "Love Me Tender."

Riding the tide of his much-lauded return, Elvis then got to work on his next film. It would be a movie that placed the real-life returning G.I. into the role of a G.I. on the silver screen for the film *G.I. Blues*. Here, Elvis plays the part of army specialist Tulsa McLean who aspires to be a famous singer. The film is full of the typical campy comedy and impromptu singing by Elvis that just about all of his theatrical productions would be known for.

The film made its debut on November 23, 1960, and was a general success at the box office raking in nearly four and a half million dollars in profits. But even better than the movie, the soundtrack, which inevitably became Elvis' next official album release, was a smash hit.

Presley was now at full production speed and was not going to slow down. His next effort was right on the heels of his last. Produced in one day at the Nashville studio in March 1961, Elvis' new album was called *Something for Everybody*. It perfectly reflected his sentiment at the time; he wished to reach out to a larger audience and bring forth something that nearly everyone could appreciate.

This album is said to perfectly showcase the so-called "Nashville sound," trading in Elvis' rugged and raw takes for a much more refined and polished production. Despite these efforts, however, from this period on, Elvis' reign as king of the music scene began to come to an end, and his hit-making potential began to decline.

From 1962 to 1965, Presley would only have three hit songs on the radio: "Return to Sender," "Viva Las Vegas," and "Crying in the Chapel," the latter of which was recorded in 1960 but wasn't released until 1965. But while his musical career was headed for the slow lane, Elvis decided to kick his personal ambition into high gear by asking his flame from his days on the army base, Priscilla, to marry him.

Chapter Nine

Comeback in Las Vegas

"You know, I had my mother and my father convincing me that he would be going back to Hollywood and he'd be back with the actresses and dating them and that he wasn't serious about me at all. So, I had him saying one thing to me and my parents telling me something else."

—Priscilla Presley

Elvis and Priscilla became husband and wife on May 1, 1967, wed at the Aladdin Hotel in Las Vegas, Nevada. The wedding ceremony was highly orchestrated and said to have been arranged by none other than Colonel Parker in order to create the biggest media buzz he could from the occasion. The wedding nuptials only lasted for eight minutes before all in attendance were herded to a breakfast reception whose creation was said to have run somewhere around $10,000.

After the reception ran its course, Elvis and his new bride hopped onto one of his personal planes and headed for Palm Springs where they spent their honeymoon. The two then returned to Memphis just a few days later on May 4. Here they retired for a time to Presley's private ranch, where they unofficially extended their honeymoon a few more days. To perhaps Priscilla's dismay, much of

Elvis' entourage, then known as the "Memphis Mafia," came to join him as well.

It was very soon into this stay that Priscilla discovered that she was pregnant. She was surprised and a little bit disappointed to become pregnant so quickly after being married. And by her own account, she even briefly considered abortion before she and Elvis both decided that they had to have their child. Their daughter, named Lisa Maria Presley, would be born almost exactly nine months to the day after Elvis and Presley were wed, coming into this world on February 1, 1968.

By that time, Elvis' career in both music and movies had significantly declined. His films were routine failures, and even the soundtracks were so dismal that they barely received radio play. More importantly, Elvis had culturally been supplanted by more relevant groups such as the Beatles and the Rolling Stones.

Elvis was becoming increasingly depressed and morose, believing that his career was over. But the ever-strategizing Colonel Parker had a plan and began talks with NBC to bring Elvis back to television in the form of what would be a Christmas special. This Christmas special was filmed in the summer of 1968, but it wouldn't air to the public until December 3 of that year. Here you could see Elvis striding the stage in a leather jumpsuit reminiscent of his glory days in the 1950s. The last time Presley had performed was, in fact, in 1961.

Elvis was said to be fairly nervous at the outset, and some say you can even see his hands shaking in the first few minutes of the broadcast. But as soon as the music started, it was vintage Presley on full display, and the ratings reflected that fact. The show proved to be the biggest draw all season for NBC and captured 42% of the total TV audience that night. In January 1969, Presley released a single from the Christmas special called "If I Can Dream," and it reached number 12 on the charts, the most traction an Elvis single had achieved in several years.

Encouraged by these results, Elvis began a recording blitz at the famed American Sound Studio in Memphis, Tennessee, which led to the celebrated album *From Elvis in Memphis*, which took the world by storm in the summer of 1969. This album featured the infective and socially conscious power ballad "In the Ghetto" which soon became a hit, reaching to number 3 on the pop charts for that year. This song was Elvis' first foray into the top ten since the early 1960s. And it wasn't the only hit; he also had great success with the songs, "Kentucky Rain," "Don't Cry Daddy," and "Suspicious Minds."

Elvis was once again in demand, and soon major venues from around the world were calling Colonel Parker, requesting Elvis to grace their stages. But it was the gigs booked in Las Vegas that really got Elvis' attention. He had been fond of the desert metropolis for quite some time, and he very much wanted to become the next big act in Sin City.

It was in Las Vegas that Elvis first started to transition his image from the leather-clad rocker to the glam jumpsuit-wearing cultural icon of his latter days. Presley was soon booked at the recently built International Hotel in the heart of Vegas, where he would perform to an audience of thousands of people. When the time came for him to perform, the crowd was largely receptive to Elvis and gave him generous rounds of applause and cheers in between each song.

Las Vegas turned out to be the perfect venue for Elvis because he could routinely perform to a large crowd of fans without having to go on backbreaking tours across the country. He found a niche in the Vegas strip that would last him until the day he died.

Chapter Ten

Last Years and Death

"It was more that his career was going down again and he was tired of the songs. He was tired of the routine. And there was a point where he just kind of gave up. He couldn't face being 40. And he resorted to stimulants. There's a dark side there, a really dark side."

—Pricilla Presley

Despite his newfound success in Vegas, when Elvis was back home in Memphis he began to behave erratically. Several members of his entourage, the Memphis Mafia, would later recall just how odd his behavior could be.

One time he insisted on taking a solo flight to Washington, D.C. to meet an ex-narcotics officer named John O'Grady. Elvis had previously hired O'Grady as a private investigator during a paternity suit and was familiar with his work in narcotics. He believed that O'Grady could help him get his own badge as a narcotics officer. Even though Elvis himself had been addicted to prescription drugs for several years, he abhorred the practice of illegal drug use. Somehow, he had developed this grandiose belief that he could put a damper on the drug problem in show business if he were given the authority to do so.

According to his close friends in the Memphis Mafia, Elvis believed that he could scare drug users straight by the power of his personality behind an official badge. He thought he would be able to clean up all the junkies from Hollywood to Memphis. It sounds far-fetched, but according to some, Elvis had already been lecturing and scaring close acquaintances out of illegal drug use by badgering them about it.

This misadventure was then followed by an impromptu visit to the White House on December 21, 1970, when Elvis walked into the place and demanded he have an audience with the president. When he received word that Elvis was waiting for him, President Richard Nixon made time to meet with the King. Nixon was surprised by the visit, but the two made the most of it, discussing their shared hatred of hippie drug culture.

Elvis then cut to the chase and asked Nixon for a Bureau of Narcotics and Dangerous Drugs badge in order to enforce his will on the drug addicts he encountered. Nixon was apparently hesitant to hand out badges to the rock legend, and so he backpedaled his way out of the discussion by explaining to Elvis that he would be much more effective if he remained undercover without an official title, using his street cred to influence the masses. After thinking about the suggestion, Elvis apparently agreed and went back to Memphis empty-handed.

More trouble was brewing back at home meanwhile, and due to several disagreements and rumored affairs between the pair, Elvis and Priscilla filed for separation in February 1972. This separation would ultimately culminate with Elvis filing for divorce on January 8, 1973, the same day as his 38th birthday.

If Elvis was much bothered by the split, he didn't show it to the public. Instead he threw himself headlong into his work, staging a first of its kind globally broadcast concert called *Aloha from Hawaii*. Elvis broadcast his performance live from Hawaii by satellite to places all over the globe. The performance was wildly popular, and the live album that was subsequently released called *Aloha from Hawaii Via Satellite* was extremely popular with his fans, and was the last hit album he would make.

Right on the heels of these accolades, Elvis' years of prescription drug use were beginning to take a toll on his body. By the end of the year, he had nearly succumbed from barbiturate overdose on two separate occasions—one of which had him put in a coma for several days. He eventually rebounded and went on tour again in 1974, but it wasn't long before he started to have a recurrence of the same old problems.

In September 1974, Elvis had several instances of passing out and falling in public, as was the case on one occasion when he rolled up to a concert at the University of Maryland only to fall flat on his face as he tried to get out of the car. Elvis was eventually convinced to see a doctor.

The physicians who examined him noted several medical problems affecting Presley's health. They discovered that he had an enlarged colon, liver dysfunction, and glaucoma in his eyes. Elvis was prescribed tinted glasses for his eyes, a new diet for his colon, and advised to quit taking drugs to save his liver. Elvis told the doctors he would heed their advice, but in the end, the only thing he took them up on was the tinted glasses.

Soon after leaving the hospital, Elvis returned to the stage in March of 1975. Elvis was now struggling with the extra weight he had gained and was often out of breath, but besides these difficulties, he was highly optimistic about getting back into the swing of things. During those opening nights in Las Vegas, he received good reviews for the most part.

Although some critics ridiculed him for his noticeable weight gain, calling him "fat and sassy," most had only good things to say about Elvis' voice and general performance. He remained in a good mood during the shows and was even able to engage in self-deprecating humor, often poking fun at his aging disposition. At one of his shows, for example, he provoked a good-natured round of laughter when he pretended to have trouble doing his classic Presley lip curl. He acted as if his lips were stiff and he couldn't get them to cooperate, before pointing to the side of his mouth and explaining, "When I was nineteen it worked just fine!" He also had fun pretending he couldn't get his legs and hips to move like they did when he was younger, acting like they were as stiff as a board and he just couldn't do the "Elvis Pelvis" routine anymore.

But in reality, it wasn't a faulty lip sneer or limited leg mobility that he had to worry about; it was his damaged liver, enlarged colon, and weakening heart function he needed to be concerned with. And in 1977, things would only go from bad to worse. By March, Elvis had to cancel several concert dates because he was unable to get out of bed. When he did manage to pull himself up and out the door, the performances he gave were often incoherent. He was found forgetting the words to his songs and almost aimlessly wandering around on stage.

The last public performance he made was on June 26, 1977, at Market Square Arena in Indianapolis, Indiana. Less than two months later, on August 16, Elvis Presley would be found dead on the floor of his bathroom.

Conclusion

Upon Elvis Presley's death, President Jimmy Carter spoke before the nation of Elvis' contributions to American society. He stated that Elvis "permanently changed the face of American popular culture." And whether you like or dislike Presley, his impact as a pop icon can hardly be denied. When he catapulted to the world stage in the late 1950s, he served as the first salvo in a culture war that never really ended.

The truth is that when some want to write off Elvis Presley and his music as outdated, cheesy, or irrelevant, they fail to recognize just how much that first display of defiant sneer and swagger changed the world.

Printed in Great Britain
by Amazon